Beyond Depression
Growing into light

Jennifer Minney

with illustrations by
Brian Minney

Silvertree Publishing

Published 2001
by
Silvertree Publishing
PO Box 2768, Yeovil, Somerset

ISBN: 0-9538446-3-3

A catalogue record for this book is available from the British Library

Printed and bound by
Bookcraft, Midsomer Norton

Author's Note

For the sake of clarity, the masculine pronoun "he" has been used throughout the book, although the text is equally, and in some cases more, applicable to women.

Contents

1

INTRODUCTION AND OVERVIEW

WHAT IS DEPRESSION?

Types of Depression

Depression is the most common emotional disturbance. According to some estimates, one in five people will experience this demoralising mental condition at some time during their lives. It is defined as a state of sadness and dejection, ranging from mild discouragement and despondency, or fits of the blues, to feelings of overwhelming hopelessness and despair. There are two main kinds of depression – reactive or clinical. But, with some exceptions, these are not two distinct types. Rather, one leads into the other, clinical depression having usually begun as a normal reaction to adverse circumstances.

Reactive Depression

Reactive depression is a response to loss of some kind. This can be anything from a momentary loss of status, like being ignored by a boss at work, to bereavement through death or divorce. In these instances, depression can be described as the soul hurting. If you fell and injured your leg you would expect your leg to hurt and be bruised. This would be normal. You would also expect the pain to lessen and the bruising to fade. In the same way, reactive depression is natural. It is only abnormal when the emotional pain is out of proportion to the cause, or when it continues longer than expected and the wounds won't heal.

Depending on the extent of the loss, reactive depression can last anything from a few hours to several months. In the case of bereavement, especially the death of a spouse, it can take up to two years to recover. But over this period the normal depression that is a part of grieving should be diminishing, and there should be periods of relative freedom from the feelings of sorrow and emptiness. If there isn't, the depression is classed as clinical, which means that medical intervention is required, perhaps in the form of antidepressants or some kind of psychological help.

Clinical Depression

With clinical depression there is a severe disturbance of mood, possibly with self-punitive wishes or thoughts of suicide, seen as a way of escape. A normal, reactive depression is likely to become more intense and debilitating when there has been a history of loss. For instance, there may have been several deaths in the family over a short period of time, a series of failed relationships, or a combination of different types of bereavement: a redundancy, a close friend moving away, a child leaving home.... Those who have experienced ongoing abuse, rejection or criticism from a spouse or near relative are especially prone to clinical depression because of the erosion of self-worth that goes with any kind of mistreatment. But the most vulnerable are those who have been abused, rejected or disapproved of in childhood.

People who, from the start, have been deprived of their most basic emotional needs do not have the resources necessary to ward off depression. Neither can they cope with the mental disturbance when it occurs. This is because a relatively minor loss in the present, such as a friend's failure to turn up for a meeting, can open up old wounds. It is like falling and hurting a leg that is already badly injured. And the pain may be excruciating.

If you have experienced any kind of emotional damage, and feel unloved and worthless as a result, this does not mean that you are doomed to spend the rest of your life being depressed, although you may be more prone to depression than others. It is possible, perhaps with the help of a counsellor or psychotherapist, to work through any residual emotional pain and find healing. This will be discussed more fully in Chapter 5. In the meantime, you can start the process by learning to understand depression, and especially your own areas of vulnerability.

WHO ARE MOST VULNERABLE TO DEPRESSION?

Women

There are several groups of people who are especially at risk of becoming depressed. One such group is women, who are twice as likely as men to experience mild depression. The reason is unknown, although some research indicates that it is primarily due to social factors, in particular the lack of an intimate or confiding relationship, or lack of social contact through work outside the home. Other environmental causes include lack of fulfilment or conflicting demands of children and work. Depression in women may also be due to hormonal or genetic causes. Or it could be because women think differently to men, using different parts of the brain, and are therefore more likely to be in touch with their emotional side, and more likely to brood on their feelings.

Creative People

Artistic people, of either gender, such as writers, painters and composers, are more likely to get depressed than people who are more technically inclined. This may be because craftsmanship of any kind is an outworking of the soul: the part of a human that is concerned with life, emotions and creative thought – as opposed to the more rational, logical thinking of the mind. In order to develop one's full creative potential it is necessary to be in tune with one's emotions and be able to channel them, and it is sometimes difficult to get the balance right: to harness and creatively express subjective feelings without being overwhelmed by them.

Spiritual People

At the deepest levels, the psychological and spiritual merge, so it is probably not surprising that people who are spiritually minded are also more prone to depression. Not only do spiritual people, like the artistic, have a deeper sense of the aesthetic, they are also more conscious of the divine in nature, as well as in themselves. The ability to respond to and enjoy beauty can be very uplifting. But, on the down side, it also makes one more aware of the ugliness of life: of wars, destruction and pollution, and the inhumanity of man to man. An awareness of the tragic loss of the original wholeness and beauty of creation can have a very depressing effect, unless it is counteracted by a healthy faith in God's goodness and continuing interest in the world, and in his power to bring good out of evil.

In the Christian Church especially, there is a danger of spiritually minded people becoming swamped by negative emotions – for several reasons. Many come to God in the first place, not only because of their heightened awareness of spiritual things, but because of past hurts, which have made them very conscious of their need for love and acceptance. So, they are already prone to depression, and their low self-esteem makes it difficult for them to accept God's love on a personal level. They tend to see themselves as exceptions: God is love, but it's everyone else he loves, not them. They are also likely to have misconceptions about God, seeing him as absent, uncaring or even abusive. Therefore they are left with a continuing sense of loneliness and exclusion, which creates yet more depression.

In addition, Christians have high standards, and when there is a failure to reach those standards, the result can be a pervasive sense of false guilt, which is one of the underlying causes of depression. This is made worse when other Christians condemn, mistakenly thinking that depression is always the result of self-pity, lack of trust or sin. The fear of condemnation, or of being given unhelpful advice, can make depressed Christians withdraw into themselves rather than seeking the help and support they need, again resulting in yet more damage to a soul that is already hurt and bruised.

Damaged People

People who have been damaged in childhood, through having been ill treated, neglected, constantly criticised and put down, or blamed for others' mistakes or unhappiness are most likely to become depressed in adulthood. This is in part because they tend to have misconceptions, not only about God, but also about other people, expecting them to be abusive, uncaring or critical. And their deep-rooted pain makes them ultra-sensitive, so they are easily hurt by any perceived rejection or censure. Moreover, when a child is deprived of his basic emotional needs for love, acceptance and approval, it sets into motion a variety of self-destruct patterns that may persist throughout life.

Sometimes the original damage goes unnoticed, making it particularly difficult to recognise and change false perceptions and destructive patterns. For instance, rough handling, tactless remarks and strained atmospheres may not have been viewed as harmful; or inappropriate or excessive physical punishment seen as abuse. And the effects of unintentional harm, especially that caused by loving parents, may have been discounted. Constantly being given reassurance when what was needed was an acknowledgment and understanding of the child's struggles and anxieties is a typical example. Also harmful is being put on a pedestal. Being worshipped by parents can be more damaging than being demeaned, because of the strain of having to live up to impossibly high standards.

With the exception of emotional damage, the very factors that make a person susceptible to depression can also be used to conquer it. So if you are emotional, whether male or female, artistic or spiritual, it is important to remember that basically these are positive attributes that can be used for good. They can, in fact, be employed to repair any residual damage to your psyche and enhance your emotional well-being. You should not try to change what, or who, you essentially are. On the contrary, being yourself, as well as knowing and understanding yourself, is vital if you are to grow out of the darkness of depression into the light of love. And knowing yourself includes being aware of your own emotional and physical responses to loss, and your own behaviour patterns.

SIGNS AND SYMPTOMS OF DEPRESSION

Emotional Signs and Symptoms

The sooner you can recognise the signs and symptoms of depression, the quicker you will be to deal with it, before it becomes severe. Signs are external indications, visible to others, of the symptoms, which are what you feel and experience inside. And the most common early symptom is a vague sensation of flatness. This is often accompanied by feelings of lethargy and tiredness, of not wanting to be bothered with anything because everything is too much effort. Later on there may be a pervasive sense of heaviness, excessive moodiness and irritability, a deep awareness of outrage, or feelings of numbness and despair. As the depression progresses, the listlessness and dejection increases until everything looks grey, and finally, black.

As the blackness takes over, feelings can no longer be aroused by former interests and pursuits. Family and friends no longer evoke warm feelings, there is a lack of appetite for food or sex, and it becomes impossible to find pleasure in anything or believe that things will ever be any different. With the lack of interest in the world around, there is a corresponding preoccupation with the dark side of life and an increasing focus on the negative aspects of oneself. There is exaggerated self-criticism and self-blame, and feelings of worthlessness and hopelessness. The sadness and despair may be experienced as a dark tunnel, with no light at the end, or a bleak, empty wilderness that goes on forever.

People experience depression in different ways, but if the tunnel, wilderness or whatever persists, there will be a desperate urge to get away from it all. A depressed person may try to escape through excessive daydreaming, living in a fantasy world. Or there may be persistent thoughts of just packing up, abandoning all responsibilities and going away somewhere, or even of committing suicide, even if this is not something that would normally be contemplated. Any, or all, of these emotional signs and symptoms may also be accompanied by physical changes.

Physical Signs and Symptoms

Physical signs and symptoms of depression have no organic cause; that is, they do not originate in the body, so they are termed psychosomatic. ("Psyche" is Greek for "soul", "soma" is Greek for "body".) Psychosomatic pain or illness is real, it is not imagined. But, because it originates in the soul, it is the soul that must first be attended to. For example, treatment may be required for grief due to a recent bereavement or for unresolved emotional trauma that occurred during childhood. If the soul-hurt is ignored or neglected and the physical symptoms allowed to persist, the body may become permanently damaged, making it more susceptible to physical pain or injury.

The most common physical symptom of depression, which may be noticeable to others, is chronic fatigue. This is made worse by sleep disturbances as constant tiredness adds to the feelings of heaviness, weakness and lack of energy. There may be difficulty getting to sleep or a tendency to keep waking in the night or too early in the morning, feeling very groggy and not yet ready to face the day. On the other hand, a depressed person may begin sleeping excessively and, however long or deeply he has slept, find it an effort to drag himself out of bed in the mornings.

Other physical signs and symptoms of depression include unexplained headaches or backache; digestive upsets, such as stomach pain, nausea or indigestion; and changes in bowel habits, perhaps accompanied by unexplained weight loss. There may be blurred vision, dryness of the mouth, a lump in the throat with difficulty swallowing, palpitations, "butterflies" in the stomach, or numbness of hands and feet. Gynaecological problems or skin eruptions may also be a result of depression. With all of these, especially the more serious illnesses, it is important to remember that they are more likely to have an organic cause, so they should be checked out; and that even if the original cause is psychological, the physical symptoms need also to be treated.

Behavioural Signs and Symptoms

Eventually, depression will also lead to behavioural changes. The classic image of a depressive is an unkempt person staring vacantly into space, speaking only occasionally in a flat, emotionless voice. This is certainly one picture. But what is more likely is that someone will continue to function, but act in ways that are out of keeping with his general character and level of efficiency. For instance, he may become sulky and complaining, or moody and bad tempered, have crying spells, often for no obvious reason, or joke excessively or inappropriately, denying that anything is wrong. He might start shutting himself away for long periods, withdrawing into his own little world, finding expression only through such things as poetry or paintings that he will be reluctant to share.

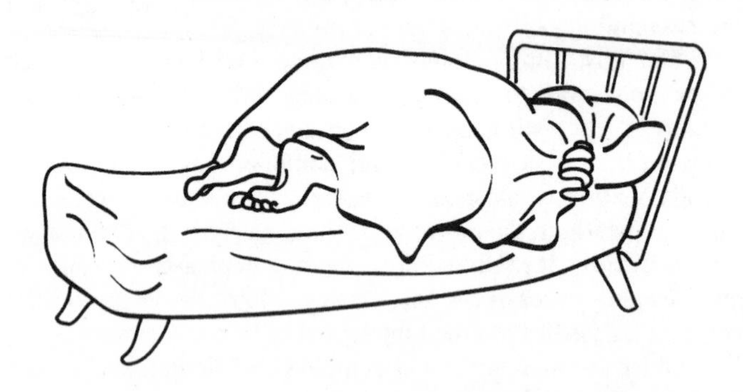

A writer may find himself writing endlessly about black tunnels, bleak deserts, or impenetrable dark mountains; stories or poems will be all about suffering and endurance, darkness and despair. An artist's paintings are likely to be dark and gloomy, lacking colour, and the entire impression may be disturbing – although, with severe depression, the artist himself might not notice it. Someone who repeatedly draws sharp, jagged lines, when normally they are soft and curving, might also be unconsciously illustrating an inner bleakness. A musician may reveal depression through sombre tunes, perhaps in the minor key, and lyrics that express feelings of hurt, rejection and loneliness.

When a depressed person emerges from his hideaway, there is likely to be a general slowing down and an inability to complete tasks he can normally take in his stride. This may be, in part, due to memory becoming less efficient, leading to difficulty concentrating. He might continue to evade responsibilities, to the extent of neglecting work, the house and children, and losing interest in personal appearance. On the other hand, he could exhibit a constant restlessness, leading to pointless over-activity. This will be more obvious to outside observers; the depressed person might not be aware that his inability to sit still, and the constant dashing around, is accomplishing very little.

The signs and symptoms of depression vary, not everyone experiences the same thing in the same order. And there is a variety in the intensity of feelings. What is important is that you recognise how depression affects you, especially in the early stages, and how it is likely to progress. When you are able to recognise the early signs and symptoms, whether emotional, physical or behavioural, you will be better able to control your depression before the depression starts controlling you – before it starts leading you to the edge of despair, and thoughts of suicide.

SOME THOUGHTS ON SUICIDE

Depression and Suicide

There appears to be no suicidal type. Thoughts of suicide, like depression, can strike anyone, regardless of age, sex, intelligence, nationality or religious belief. And the most common cause of suicide is depression. Thoughts of killing oneself arise when the emotional pain becomes unbearable and it seems that it will go on for ever, or when negative thoughts about oneself become so pervasive that death appears to be the only possible option. This distorted view of self leads to the mistaken belief that death will release others, as well as oneself, from an intolerable burden, and often the only thing preventing suicide is a strong belief in God. But depression can distort thinking to such an extent that even committed Christians become convinced that God doesn't care – or even that he doesn't exist. Ideally, help should have been sought before depression reaches this stage. But even in the deepest depression there are likely to be periods of lucidity when it is possible to think clearly about suicide, and what it will achieve.

Reasons for Suicide Attempts

A suicide attempt is often a cry for help; a last, desperate attempt to communicate. It is difficult to explain what it's like being depressed, to get across just how painful and debilitating it is, and to make matters worse, people generally don't understand depression. So, however well it is explained, they don't grasp its seriousness. If someone has a broken leg, family and friends would normally be sympathetic; they would try to make life easier, doing the running around while the leg healed, and they would most likely be extra caring, bringing, flowers, providing those little touches that mean so much when life gets tough. But they can't see depression. And if they have never been depressed they are likely to respond with an impatient, "Come on, pull yourself together," or "Snap out of it." A suicide bid may, then, be an attempt to make depression tangible and understandable, to demonstrate the severity of the emotional pain, in the hope of receiving care and assistance.

A suicide attempt may also be a cry for revenge. When others have hurt you it is an instinctive reaction to want to hurt them in return. And when thought patterns are very disturbed, a depressed person, and especially a teenager, may think that his suicide will enable him to get his own back. He will be incapable of thinking rationally, or with any compassion, about the terrible and often permanent devastation suicide wreaks on those left behind. Instead, there will be the irrational belief that he will somehow be there, present at his own funeral, to enjoy their suffering and remorse.

With teenagers in particular, suicide can be a cry for happiness. They expect instant solutions to life's problems and fail to understand that it is normal to sometimes feel unhappy, and that bad times pass. There is, therefore, a very real danger that they will succeed in their suicide attempt, not necessarily because of the extent of their depression, but because of their low tolerance to frustration and pain. The danger is exacerbated by their tendency to view suicide in a romantic light; they don't understand, or are unfamiliar with, the process of death.

Finally, suicide may be a cry for peace. When this cry is the loudest it is then that someone is likely to go through with it. These people fully intend to kill themselves because they want to put an end to all their turmoil and confusion, and they can't see any other way. They think, falsely, that suicide will solve all their problems, refusing to consider the biblical truth that death is not the end; that they will have to face their Maker and explain why they didn't want his precious gift of life, and why they couldn't trust him to meet their needs. Suicide is not the answer to depression; the reality is very different.

The Reality of Suicide

A very high proportion of suicide attempts fail, leaving the sufferer in a worse condition than before. For example, an overdose of drugs, such as aspirin, sedatives, amphetamines and barbiturates, can cause, among other things, permanent brain damage – as can an unsuccessful hanging. Slashes to the wrist can result in irreparable nerve damage, severely restricting the use of the hand; caustics cause severe burns, with persistent scarring; and falling from heights can result in lifelong disability.

In addition to the physical damage caused by a suicide attempt, there is an increase, rather than a resolution, of the problems that led to the attempt in the first place. For instance, many institutions won't employ people who have tried killing themselves, and some insurance companies won't insure them, while acquaintances may start treating them as if they are crazy or dangerous, leading to greater isolation.

If a suicide attempt is successful, death may, in fact, be just the beginning of their problems. Man is destined to die once, and after that to face judgement.[1] There is a lot of controversy regarding whether or not suicide is the unforgivable sin, and unanswered questions about what happens to Christians who commit suicide. The questions are particularly fraught when the suicidal has lived an exemplary life, devoted to God, involved in the community and his local church, and committed to his family who, excepting his depressed state and violent end, remember him with gratitude and love.

Perhaps it would be more helpful to look at the question of suicide in the context of psychological and spiritual growth. God wants us to grow and develop in love: to learn, through his love, how to love ourselves and others, to discover our unique strengths and abilities and realise our full potential. What suicide does is prevent the possibility of any further development. So the suicidal has to face God in an unfinished state, never having become what he might and should have been. This is the real sin of suicide, and it brings its own judgement.

Suicide, Depression and Self-development

While suicide permanently halts any further development of the self; severe or prolonged depression slows it down, making self-actualisation far more difficult than it need be. Depression is a crippling disease of the mind and soul, robbing us of peace and preventing us from fully being alive, from being what God intended us to be. It is for this reason that merely finding ways of alleviating the symptoms of depression is not enough. In order to realise our full potential, we have to grow beyond depression, making it essentially a thing of the past.

Growing beyond depression does not mean that you will never be down or discouraged again. Remember, depression is a normal response to loss, and some people are more susceptible than others. But it is possible to find ways of protecting yourself from its most debilitating effects, and to ensure that depression never again dominates your life. But before you go forward you must first look back, to discover and understand the underlying causes, as well as the current triggers, and to recognise how you may be repeating childhood patterns and causing your own moods of sadness and despair.

2

THE CAUSES OF DEPRESSION

CURRENT FACTORS

The Question of Causes

Depression can have a variety of causes: physical, spiritual or psychological. However, it is impossible to divide ourselves up into three distinct parts, and unhelpful even to try. We were created an integrated whole, and damage to one part of the self also affects the other parts. It is also impossible to say exactly where in a person's being depression begins. For instance, it is recognised that depression slows down the brain's functioning, but it is not known whether a person becomes depressed because of the changes in the brain, or whether the brain changes are a result of the depression. Bearing this in mind, we will now look at three main sources of depression.

Physical Causes

Physical, or organic, causes of depression can be further divided into four main groups. The first includes brain damage as a result of accident or injury; brain tumour, which would give rise to other symptoms, like constant severe headache; and brain disease, such as meningitis or encephalitis. In these instances, the depression is cured as the underlying cause is dealt with, so for the purposes of this book can be excluded.

Depression may also be caused by toxins (poisons), the classic examples being drugs and alcohol. A GP will inform a patient if any prescription drugs are likely to cause depression. Over-the-counter drugs also contain information about possible side effects. The main problem is likely to come from illegal drugs, or a combination of drugs. But the most common toxin in connection with depression is alcohol. Depressed people often drink to blot out painful feelings and make themselves feel better.

However, alcohol is itself a depressant; it depresses, or damps down, the central nervous system. So, after the immediate boost that alcohol gives, a person is left feeling worse.

A third group of physical causes is disturbances in blood chemistry, such as blood sugar levels. Diabetics, for instance, may have bouts of mild depression if the diabetes is not properly controlled. Depression can also be caused by unhealthy eating habits, in particular a tendency to binge on sweet things, or to go on crash diets. Other blood chemistry disturbances, which may also be brought about by crash dieting, include water balance or acid-alkali ratio. It is unlikely that these will be the only cause of depression; more usually they will exacerbate an already existing one. But learning to eat healthily can help bring depression under control.

The most common physical cause of depression, especially in women, is endocrine (hormonal) disturbance. This can give rise to pre-menstrual tension (PMT), post-natal depression (PND), and menopausal depression. If PMT is a problem, it might help to keep a menstrual chart so that off-days can be anticipated and planned for. But PMT, like other physical causes, is not likely to be the only factor involved. What usually happens is that a vague feeling of sadness or despondency because of life's circumstances becomes more acute at this time, and less easy to deal with. The same applies for PND and menopausal depression, although both of these have their own built-in problems. Physical causes of depression will also aggravate any feelings of oppression arising from spiritual issues.

Spiritual Causes

It is especially difficult to separate soul (or psyche) – which is the thinking/feeling part of self – and spirit: that part of a human which tends him towards God and enables him to commune with God. But there are three causes of depression that are essentially spiritual. The first is an uneasy conscience because of behaviour that is known to be wrong. This is true guilt, as opposed to the false guilt that tends to dog someone's footsteps when there has been a history of abuse. True guilt can easily be identified in that it has a specific cause, and the guilt is in proportion to the cause. True guilt, like physical pain, is a warning that something is wrong. And the result, if the guilt is ignored and the harmful behaviour continued, is a feeling of heaviness and unease. This is because, apart from the effect sin has on our relationship with God and anyone we may have hurt, it violates our own standards – if it didn't, there wouldn't be any feeling of guilt. And it is this impairment of self-integrity that ultimately leads to depression.

Another spiritual cause of depression is an unwillingness to forgive. Forgiveness is not the same as reconciliation: it takes two to reconcile, and when there has been abuse it may not be in the victim's, or perpetrator's, best interests. Forgiveness is a process that involves working through the hurt and anger until there is an ability to let go of the desire for revenge or restitution. Being unable to forgive because of not having reached the stage of letting go is different from being unwilling to forgive. When there is an obdurate refusal to forgive, then the natural and just anger that is felt as a result of someone else's wrongdoing turns into bitterness. And bitterness destroys; it erodes the self, and this self-destruction is often experienced as a deep sense of sadness and despair.

Involvement in the occult can also lead to depressed feelings. With a very few exceptions, God has given us the entire universe to explore; he wants us to be curious, to search out, question, and discover new things. But just as a loving parent would allow a toddler to explore a house that had been rendered safe but place a gate at the kitchen door to prevent the child being burned on a hot stove, so God has set boundaries around the world of the occult. Becoming involved in things like witchcraft, spiritualism, Satanism, astrology, ouija boards and the like opens us up to evil influences, and one of the most common effects is a persistent feeling of oppression – like being under a permanent dark cloud.

When depression has a spiritual cause, the remedy is relatively straightforward and can bring immediate relief. It usually involves changing an attitude or behaviour, or implementing a course of action, such as apologising to someone we may have hurt. But when depression has a psychological cause, being a reaction to circumstances that may be outside of our control, it is not so easy to overcome.

Psychological Causes

Anyone, regardless of age, can experience loss, with the associated feelings of depression. But just as different age groups are vulnerable to particular kinds of physical illnesses, so does each stage of life create a susceptibility to specific kinds of loss. We will look at a few examples, beginning with babies and small children. Even they can get depressed, usually because of exposure to family conflict, or through being neglected or abused. In all these cases, the child experiences the loss of a secure environment, as well as the absence of a parent – the mother or father is emotionally unavailable even if physically present – and this results in feelings of insecurity, fear and deep unhappiness.

Adolescents who are going through puberty are prone to depression, in part because of hormonal changes, but also because of their rapid physical changes: the loss of the body they knew and were comfortable with. There are also major cognitive changes, when thinking becomes less concrete and more abstract. This results in the blurring of what was considered a fixed and certain identity. Adolescence is a time of questioning, doubting and reaffirming the self; letting go of childhood and finding new directions. Also at this time, teenagers reflect more on what could be and might have been, so they become disillusioned with parents, society, and the world at large. In addition, adolescents may have to contend with failed exams, conflict with parents, or being let down by friends of the opposite sex.

Young adults, in their twenties and thirties, may become depressed because of family responsibilities or issues around child-rearing, including difficulties conceiving, miscarriage, abortion or baby loss. Young mothers especially may have a pervading sense of emptiness because of having had to give up work and adjust to a new role. The loss of status and financial and social freedom is felt even when the new baby is wanted and very much loved. The depressed feelings may be exacerbated by the hormonal changes that occurred with pregnancy and childbirth. In addition, having a baby triggers memories, which may not be conscious, of one's own babyhood and experience of being parented. If this has been inadequate, old wounds will be opened, reactivating the more deep-rooted causes of depression. Young men, on the other hand, are more likely to become depressed because of difficulties at work, such as losing a contract or not getting an expected promotion. Moving to a new area, especially if this involves leaving family or close friends, can likewise lead to depression.

Middle-aged people are more vulnerable to depression than any other group. This is the age when people tend to look back and assess what they have accomplished in life, and there may be the realisation that it is not actually very much. This is also the time when children leave home. The empty nest syndrome is most likely to trigger depression in a woman if she has given up a career to bring up her family and has no other interests. And hormonal changes caused by the menopause will add to the depressed feeling. Being made redundant is especially devastating in middle age when there is less likelihood of finding alternative work; and the loss of employment, status and income may lead to feelings of anxiety, worthlessness and even despair.

Elderly people commonly get depressed because of physical problems, with the associated curtailing of mobility. The sense of deprivation will be particularly acute if they have had to give up something they really enjoyed, such as gardening, DIY or sewing. Also, the loss of independence, especially in someone who has always been autonomous, deeply erodes the sense of self; and this, combined with feelings of uselessness and purposelessness, is particularly depressing. In addition, elderly people have to cope with retirement and the loss of loved ones through death.

Depression, then, has a variety of causes, affecting different people at different times. But, as has been noted, some are generally more susceptible than others: women and people who are artistically or spiritually inclined. It has also been remarked that those particularly at risk are damaged people, especially if the harm occurred in childhood, because emotional deprivation in the early developmental years produces a gap in the child's psyche, leaving him without the reserves needed to deal with life's problems. It may also create feelings that are so overpowering they are pushed deep inside where, like a tumour, they eat away at the self, causing yet more extensive damage.

If you are prone to depression, it may be that you have failed to recognise any early damage, or disregarded it, telling yourself that, since it is in the past, you just have to forget it and get on with life. But there has to be a resolution, or healing, of past hurts in order to deal effectively with the present. For easier identification, these root causes will be divided into four main areas. If you have experienced any kind of trauma in childhood, or been deprived of love, affection or approval, you will probably identify all four as relevant to your own struggles, because the four are mutually dependent.

ROOT CAUSES

Damaged Self-esteem

The foundations of self-esteem are developed during childhood, and any damage occurring during this time will, if untreated, lead to patterns of thinking and behaviour that will invite and prolong depression. A healthy self-esteem means, basically, that a person has a true sense of his own worth, secure in the knowledge that he is loved, accepted and approved, and he will be able to realistically assess his strengths and weaknesses, utilise his strengths and work at overcoming his weaknesses. He will also be able to form healthy relationships.

Self-esteem may be damaged during childhood through abuse, rejection or constant disapproval. These make children feel that they are bad: that there must be something very wrong with them — although, at the same time, they know that they are not at fault. Sexual abuse in particular can have this confusing effect, even if it was mild or happened only once. It also gives mixed messages about the child's value. The surface communication might be, "I love you." But the underlying message is, "You are just there to be used; your feelings don't count." Confusion is particularly severe if, as is usual, the abuser is someone the child loves and respects.

The feeling of not being essentially good, valuable and approved erodes self-esteem to such an extent that children who have survived the actual abuse may grow up to discover that there is really no escape. They can't put the past behind them because they are still struggling to believe in their own worth and trust their own judgements and abilities. At times they may succeed, at others they can easily feel undermined by others, and the old voices begin again in their heads, telling them that they are no good, they're not worth anything, they can't get anything right. These thoughts and feelings inevitably lead to depression.

Rejection has a similar effect. When parents, or other significant adults, reject a child, perhaps because he wasn't planned or was the wrong sex, or has some disability, the child will grow up feeling like an outcast. He will feel different, and probably not know why. So right from the start there will be a deep consciousness of sadness and regret. This will be particularly severe when the rejection has been more overt, perhaps through the parents actually saying that the child isn't wanted, or through sending him away against his will or throwing a teenager out onto the street. A child will, to some extent, also feel rejected if parents separate or divorce, if the break-up is not handled sensitively, or if he is replaced in a parent's affections by a new step-parent or sibling.

Rejection can also come from peers, in the form of teasing, bullying, or being excluded from gangs or friendship circles. Changing schools can be very traumatic for some children, especially if they are very shy and withdrawn, or if the changes are frequent or occur at critical times, such as prior to exams. As a result of the trauma, they may develop a persistent feeling of never quite fitting in. But whether the rejection comes from family members, teachers, other significant adults, or peers, the ensuing sadness may be so pervasive that the sufferer loses touch with it, just as one can forget a nagging physical pain. He will then wonder why he reacts so badly to a friend ignoring him, or being turned down for a job. The sadness of rejection lays a very solid foundation for subsequent depression.

Ongoing disapproval in childhood also erodes self-esteem. Parents, teachers and the like can show this in many ways, the most obvious being through constant criticism. For example, telling a child that he is stupid or ugly will make him grow up with a deep insecurity, making him very dependent on the opinions of others. And he will easily be cast down if others don't approve. But criticism may be more subtle, through, for instance, giving backhanded compliments, or focusing on, or drawing attention to, the negative. Statements like, "You did well, but..." are guaranteed to deflate a child's sense of self-worth. Comparing a child unfavourably with others, or making unrealistic demands, leading to inevitable failure, will likewise damage a child's self-esteem, making him more susceptible to depression in later life. Feelings of insignificance and failure, from whatever cause, will also give rise to anger.

Repressed Anger

Children who are abused or rejected, or who are constantly put down, naturally become angry. The anger comes from feeling hurt, betrayed, let down, abandoned, rejected.... It comes also from feeling helpless and vulnerable, and from a sense of injustice, of having been treated unfairly. The most anger may be directed at a parent who failed to protect, or at society's or God's failure to intervene, and it can be so overwhelming that it has to be suppressed: that is, consciously pushed down. In time,

a person may develop the habit of doing this unconsciously; the anger is then repressed. And it is this build-up of unrecognised anger that is often at the root of depression.

People suppress, and later repress, anger for many reasons. They may, for instance, have been brought up in a hostile environment and be afraid of violence – which is a destructive expression of anger. The fear will be especially strong if they have been subjected to, or witnessed, abuse, threats, shouting and yelling, or frequent arguments. Or they may have been told that their anger, rather than their temper tantrums, was wrong, and perhaps even punished for it. When parents are unable to tolerate outbursts of rage because of their own insecurities, children may feel the need to quash their feelings for fear of hurting their parents. Or, they may not be able to understand why they feel angry about a loving parent's decision – to move house, re-marry, or whatever – and so feel guilty. In all these cases, the children may not be able to admit even to themselves that they are angry.

Christians especially may have a mistaken belief that all anger is wrong, even though we are told not to sin in our anger,[2] and Jesus himself expressed anger on many occasions. Or they may perhaps allow for "righteous anger", interpreting this to mean anger on someone else's behalf, but not permit personal anger – although there is actually no difference. Anger is a normal human emotion; a reaction to hurt or injustice, whether directed at others or oneself. It is a very powerful form of energy and, like any other form, such as electricity, can be used for good or evil – so, in itself is neither right nor wrong, righteous nor unrighteous.

Anger is healthy when it has a cause, when it is in proportion to the cause, and when it is used to bring about positive change. But when anger is allowed to turn into bitterness, or a vindictive desire for revenge, it becomes self-destructive – as well as harming others. It eats away at a person, preventing him from living life to the full. Similarly, anger that is denied or unrecognised can be turned in upon oneself. In both cases, the most common symptom is depression, which is intensified when there is also a pervasive sense of guilt, perhaps for being angry in the first place.

False Guilt

Children who have been abused or rejected, constantly criticised or falsely condemned, and children who cannot measure up to their parents' or teachers' expectations and demands, tend to feel guilty – and without cause. They are not guilty; they have done nothing wrong. But it is difficult for children to believe this because they see their parents as perfect and teachers as all-knowing. They really only begin to question adults with the onset of the cognitive changes that occur during adolescence. Because children are unable to perceive adults, especially parents, as being at fault, they blame themselves, telling themselves that if only they were prettier, or tried harder, they would be loved and approved. By the time they are able to recognise that it is their parents, or other significant adults, who have problems, not themselves, the feeling of guilt may be so deep-rooted that it is no longer fully recognised, so is never fully discarded.

Feelings of guilt are particularly evident when there been a history of sexual abuse. They arise not only because of children thinking that they, not the abusers, must be to blame, but because they failed to stop the mistreatment, protect a sibling, or report the exploitation. Or, conversely, there may be guilt because of reporting it and being the means of breaking up the family. A sexually abused child may blame himself for being in the wrong place at the wrong time, for wearing the wrong clothes, acting seductively.... But whatever the cause of guilt, it tends to continue into adult life, not only because of deep-rooted perceptions of being inferior or different, but also because of the tendency to assume responsibility for everyone else's feelings. This is an unrealistic and impossible task, and the inevitable failures lead to yet more guilt, and an ever-increasing propensity to see oneself in a negative and hopeless light.

False guilt, which is feeling guilty for things you haven't done or for others' failings and shortcomings, can easily become all-pervasive, and eventually unrecognised, because there is no remedy – short of rejecting it. Confession or reparation can bring no relief, so there is a constant feeling of heaviness, and a vague sense of impending doom. And this exacerbates another root cause of depression – fear.

Generalised Fear

Children who are brought up in a hostile or rejecting environment, who are subjected to abuse or witness abuse, or who are punished for failing to reach their parents' impossible standards, are likely to grow up feeling afraid. This may be fear of the abuser or dictator: fear of being in his presence, of saying or doing something that will trigger physical violence, or fear of threats being carried out. With sexual abuse there may be anxiety about being damaged inside, and often there is apprehension about disclosing abuse and not being believed, as well as the fear of being perceived as bad or crazy.

At first the fear will be normal: a healthy response to a threatening person, such as a physically abusive father, or a dangerous situation. But, if untreated, the fear is likely to become generalised. There may then, for example, be a feeling of unease around all men or authority figures; or a sense of panic in any situation or place that triggers the fearful memory. A generalised anxiety can also arise from being constantly criticised, humiliated or demeaned, especially by parents or teachers. So there may be a reluctance to try anything new, or to start up a conversation with a stranger, for fear of getting it wrong or saying the wrong thing.

When fear becomes all-consuming it fails to serve its normal, useful function: to make one avoid the dangerous person or situation. Instead, it has a crippling effect, preventing the development of one's true self. A fearful person feels inhibited, lacking freedom and spontaneity, and he is kept back from reaching, or even making, goals for the future. Fear keeps a person trapped in his own little world, and this confinement of the soul in a dark, unvarying prison of its own making is the very essence of depression.

If, as a child, you were abused or rejected, constantly put down, or exalted too highly with impossible demands made on you, then you will need to deal with the root causes of your depression – low self-esteem, anger, guilt and fear – as well as learning how to cope with current triggers. Only then will you be able to grow beyond depression. You will also need to start recognising how you may be repeating the patterns of your childhood by abusing, rejecting or condemning yourself.

REPEATED PATTERNS

The Pattern of Self-abuse

When there has been abuse in childhood, or any other emotional trauma, the feeling of being bad or worthless, and the anger, guilt and fear all combine to produce a tendency to self-harm. The desire to abuse oneself will usually be unconscious and manifested through such things as self-induced stress, brought about by unnecessary time pressure, work or contact overload. It may also be shown in a tendency to overburden the self with others' problems; an inability to switch off, leading to constant exhaustion; and depression itself. Or, it may be revealed through psychosomatic symptoms, such as high blood pressure, migraines or stomach ulcers. When the desire to hurt oneself is conscious, it will be exhibited through such things as verbal beatings, various forms of physical self-mutilation and persistent thoughts of suicide.

However, the tendency to self-harm may be more subtle. For example, someone might unconsciously sabotage his own work prospects through forgetting appointments or turning up late for important meetings. He will then get depressed because of having been passed over. Or, he may act in ways that cause retaliatory anger in relatives or friends, or drive people away, resulting in loneliness and hurt, again damaging the self. He may unconsciously punish himself for perceived wrongdoing by repeatedly getting involved in destructive relationships, or through placing himself in situations where he is likely to be harmed. In all these cases, the feelings of being attacked, ignored or disliked will deepen any existing depression, and reinforce another destructive pattern: that of self-rejection.

The Pattern of Self-rejection

Someone who has been emotionally damaged during the developmental years, for whatever reason, is likely to have distorted perceptions of himself, others, the world in general and God. The distortions will begin with himself: he will not see himself, and therefore not be able to accept himself, as he really is. He may perhaps think that he isn't as intelligent as others, or that he is physically inferior, or he may see himself as a non-achiever, someone who can never quite get it right. This constant self-rejection not only erodes the self, it leads to isolation and loneliness, which in turn leads to a greater propensity to focus on oneself and one's own shortcomings, making depression more tenacious and harder to shake off than ever.

Constant introspection, and the difficulty finding anything good about oneself, is typical of depression. Also in keeping is the tendency to discount positive self-attributes and good personal experiences, while seeing others as having everything. Powerful or successful people especially will be idealised, perceived as all-good; that is, until they are discovered to be human. Then they will be seen as all-bad and will be either attacked (usually verbally) or avoided. Similarly with God. If God doesn't act in the way expected, he is likely to be seen as incapable or uncaring. As a result, a strong faith that may have provided a shield from the most debilitating effects of depression will be seriously damaged. There will also be a sense of estrangement from God, as well as from other people and oneself, leading to yet more loneliness and yet more depression.

Self-rejection is akin to self-avoidance: a fear of looking inside and seeing one's true self, so that parts of the self, usually the good parts, are denied. The result is stunted psychological and spiritual growth. However, when it is the negative aspects that are disowned, they tend to break through in unexpected and destructive ways, like feelings of panic in non-threatening situations, or outbursts of uncontrolled rage. Avoiding, and denying, the reality of self also makes it more difficult to face up to external realities. For instance, there may be denial of a disability, deteriorating relationship, or financial trouble, with a subsequent failure to address the problem; or an inability to recognise abuse, with the result that it isn't stopped. What is perceived as reactive depression, a normal response to loss, may actually be more complex. The external circumstances may be caused by the depression, rather than the other way round. And the perpetual failure to cope with life's circumstances will increase any tendency to self-criticism and blame.

The Pattern of Self-condemnation

When children are constantly criticised, or made to feel that they don't measure up, they are likely to do one of two things. Either they will keep striving, trying to be perfect in the hope that they will gain approval, or they will give up. In both cases there is a continuous feeling of frustration and disappointment, with a corresponding depressed mood. Perfectionists are never satisfied with themselves, and any performance that falls short of the ideal is likely to be seen as total failure. They will then judge themselves very harshly, and condemn themselves for their perceived inadequacy. A person who doesn't try may tell himself that he doesn't care, but he too will feel that he has failed in life.

Perfectionists tend also to label themselves rather than their performance. For instance, they will think, "I am a failure," rather than "I didn't do so well with that." Or, "I am stupid," rather than, "That was a daft thing to do." They are also prone to guilt and anxiety if they don't continue to live up to their parents' standards, being convinced that they and others disapprove of them or have negative thoughts about them. The sense of condemnation may be so pervasive that they blame themselves for others' feelings or failings, or even for some external event with which they can have no possible connection. These persistent feelings of being judged and condemned are perfect ingredients for depression.

If you have realised that, in addition to current losses and difficulties, your depression is also caused by deep-rooted hurts, and that you have continued the patterns of childhood by abusing, rejecting and condemning yourself, the recognition itself can begin the process of releasing you from the past. This in turn will enable you to grow beyond depression, so that it is no longer a major factor in your life. But it is important to remember that growth takes time. There will not be a change overnight, so be patient with yourself. Remember also that you are not alone. Throughout history, people of all ranks and kinds have battled with depression, including Bible characters: godly men and women who, like us, have struggled with the question of pain and suffering, and striven to find light in the darkness. They have left us a legacy of hope, showing us the way to wholeness and health.

3

EXAMPLES AND INSPIRATION

HOW OTHERS CAN HELP

Giving Reassurance

When we get depressed, there is a tendency to feel isolated, in part because of the difficulty explaining depression to those who have never experienced it. And the loneliness not only increases the feelings of sadness and despondency, it also creates fear. We start to feel that there must be something terribly wrong with us, that we are inadequate, weak or unspiritual. It helps, therefore, to know that someone else has felt the same way, especially if that someone else is successful, powerful, or highly respected. It is reassuring and comforting, and makes us feel that we are not as alone in the world as we thought.

Ideally, there should be someone in the family to turn to, or a close friend. But it can also be a relief to discover that people throughout history have experienced exactly the same symptoms of depression, shown the same signs, and eventually recovered. Reading about others who have been through the dark valley of depression, and come out the other end, enables us to put depression into perspective, to recognise it as universal and not peculiar to the twenty-first century. It also reassures us that we are not bad, weak, or going crazy, and that the depression will pass.

Producing Solidarity

When others, past or present, not only admit to having been depressed, but openly and honestly share the depth of their pain and confusion, we also have a sense of solidarity, a feeling that there is someone on our side. A classic example is the Psalmist David. On one occasion especially, he was going through a bad time: he was being harassed by his enemies, he was angry and grieved at all the wickedness around him, and he was troubled by his own thoughts and swamped by his own negative emotions. Not surprisingly, it all got too much for him, and he prayed for the wings of a dove, so that he could fly away and be at rest, in a place of shelter, far from the tempest and storm. [3]

The desperate wish, "If only I could just pack my things and go away somewhere," is so typical of depression that many will readily identify with David's prayer. His yearning to escape validates our own feelings, and there is a conviction that, were David alive today, he would be someone we could talk to. He would understand and know how to respond.

We would also be able to talk to the prophet, Jonah. He was a good man with a lot of repressed anger who experienced just one frustration too many. He had tried unsuccessfully to run away, avoiding what he knew in his heart was the right course for him. He'd been half drowned, he'd spent three days and nights in the belly of a great fish, and he'd then been the means of God sparing his country's enemy, when he'd much rather they'd been wiped out. As if that wasn't enough, the tropical leafy plan under which he was sheltering from the fierce sun shrivelled up and died. At this point, he prayed that God would take away his life, because he thought it would be better to die than live. [4]

How much more constructive it is to know that a great prophet like Jonah got so depressed that he felt suicidal, or to hear a friend say with feeling and understanding, "I struggled too when I was depressed," than a well-meaning command to snap out of it, or a pious exhortation to just trust the Lord.

Hearing, or reading, that someone else has been there and can reach out to us in empathy is soothing for the soul. It is also an inspiration. We can learn from their experiences, finding ways of coping with depression and overcoming it.

Providing Guidance

When others have been through depression, it is useful to discover how they reacted, how their friends responded, what they found the most comforting, and how they eventually found peace and happiness. When Job experienced a series of catastrophic events that wiped out his family and destroyed his possessions, his wife was no help whatsoever, telling him to curse God and die — although it must be remembered that she had experienced the same losses. His friends, on the other hand, were helpful, up to a point. On seeing Job they wept, and for seven days they just sat there in silence, saying not a word but quietly sharing his grief and confusion. This was exactly what he needed. When depression goes deep, silent sympathy can be the greatest balm.

Elijah's needs were met in a different way. Following his great triumph at Carmel when he had called down fire from heaven, proving that his God was greater than Baal, he had run away, terrified for his life because of the threats of Queen Jezebel. As he sat under a broom tree in the desert praying for death, an angel touched him and provided food and drink. Sometimes in depression all that is needed is a friendly touch, a hug, a cooked meal, or some other practical assistance. At other times, like Job, what is most required is silent sympathy; or, like Jonah, a stern talking to and appeal to rational thought. There are also occasions when, in company with David, expressing thoughts and feelings through music or poetry provides the comfort necessary.

You will probably have identified with some, if not all, of the people mentioned. And you may have experienced your own helpful angel, Job's comforters, or challenging voice from heaven. Or perhaps there has been no one to stand by you and understand, and although you have found consolation in poetry or music, or in keeping a journal, you have longed for the company and warmth of another human being. This longing is normal and healthy. We were never meant to be alone. But, in order to obtain the help you require from others, you must be aware of your needs and be able to express them. Often, friends and relatives want to be supportive, but they don't know how.

Of the examples cited, those who most struggled with depression were Job and David, so we will now look at their experiences more closely to see how their needs were met, and how they subsequently recovered from their depression and feelings of suicide. We will also turn to someone not yet mentioned — Rebekah. Very little is said about her depression, or how she overcame it; but, as a mother struggling with children who didn't turn out as she'd hoped, she is someone with whom many will identify. We will begin with the most ancient of stories: that of the patriarch, Job.

A PHILOSOPHER'S QUESTIONS

Job's Losses

Job was a moral, upright man with a big family, and he was very rich, his wealth consisting of large herds of various livestock. Then he suffered a series of catastrophes, one quickly following the other. First, there was an attack by Arabs who, having killed his workers, carried off his donkeys and oxen. Then there was a lightning strike which wiped out his entire flock of sheep. Then a raiding party of Chaldeans stole his camels. And finally a whirlwind killed his entire family of seven sons and three daughters who were celebrating together in the house of the eldest. Job was subsequently struck down with a painful attack of boils, which covered his entire body. It is generally thought that this was a staphylococcal infection. If so, it was probably a psychosomatic illness brought on by extreme stress. Job had lost everything! Only his wife was left, and all she could do was tell him to curse God and die.

Job's Comforters

The term, "Job's comforter", has come to mean someone who is of little or no help in time of trouble. But, in fact, Job's friends, unlike his wife, were at first very supportive. Three of them, Eliphaz, Bildad and Zophar, set off immediately from their homes to be with Job, and they were so shocked by his changed appearance that they sat down and wept. In times of extreme grief, when words are so inadequate, this is often the best thing anyone can do. They also helped with their silence. For seven days they said nothing; they just sat with Job, keeping him company and reaching out to him in love and empathy. In the end, it was Job who broke the silence with a painful outburst in which he cursed the day of his birth, wishing he had never been born. [5]

It was then that the three friends, and a young man, Elihu, who had joined them later, tried to help Job find answers and make sense of his calamities. They were attempting to find some consistent pattern that would enable them to explain human suffering; and, with the possible exception of Elihu, they thought perhaps the pattern was one of cause and effect. They reasoned that suffering must always be due to personal sinfulness, and they all, in turn, launched into long-winded discourses to that effect — which were no help whatsoever but rather added to Job's misery. They were not trying to put Job down. They were, in fact, wise, godly and very caring men. But they were speaking from their own very limited knowledge and experience.

When they failed to convince Job that his suffering was a result of direct sin, Elihu tried a different track, reasoning that God deliberately used suffering to mould character. But the thought that God had brought calamity on him because he had been chosen to endure suffering, perhaps with the purpose of helping others, was equally repugnant to Job. Again, his friends' ideas were too simplistic. They didn't go deep enough or far enough. They did not have the entire picture.

Job's Restoration

Suffering is a fact of life, and there is often no rhyme nor reason to it. And this is the conclusion that Job and his comforters eventually reached. Job's help did not come from all their reasoning and logic. It came from their humbly accepting the limitations of their understanding and looking at the larger picture. It came when he was challenged to look around him: to see himself in relation to God and his creation, and the brevity of human existence in the context of eternity.

As Job contemplated the stars and pondered the miracle of the changing seasons; as he reflected on the wonders of the earth and sea; as he marvelled at natural phenomena, such as snow, hail, rain and lightning; and as he considered the great diversity of reptile and animal life, Job admitted that it was all too much for him to grasp and understand. And he stopped trying to come up with simplistic answers. But paradoxically, it was as he renounced the efficacy of human reasoning to explain the mystery of sin and suffering, through becoming aware of his own smallness and sinfulness in comparison with God, that he gained a greater sense of his own integrity and worth and a greater ability to trust God. It also enabled him to take his eyes off his own problems and develop a concern for others, with the result that his material wealth was restored and he was given, over time, a new family.

It doesn't always happen that losses are restored. But Job's story is one that is relevant to all people at all times because it speaks to a universal need. We all experience loss, and we all try to come up with answers. And we have all received ill-contrived advice from family and friends, like, "You wouldn't be depressed if you left that partner — if you got yourself a job — if you prayed more," or the equally unhelpful, "You must be very special to have been allowed to go through that. God has some special purpose for you." It is not wrong or unhealthy to try to reason things out; on the contrary, we have been given minds that are meant to be used. But we must accept that there are no easy answers, and we must put ourselves back in touch, not only with other people, but also with the whole created world. It is only as we rediscover our place and role in the cosmos, and thereby put suffering in perspective, that depression shrinks to a more manageable size.

A MOTHER'S DISTRESS

Rebekah's Troubles

Rebekah, the wife of Isaac, son of the patriarch Abraham, seemed to have difficulty working out her role in her immediate family, never mind the universe. And her losses were very different to Job's. But she too reached the point of hopelessness and despair, and wished for death. She had spent the first twenty years of her marriage trying to get pregnant, which must have been utterly demoralising for her, eating away at her self-esteem and making her question why God had chosen her to be the wife of this very important man. But at last she gave birth to twin boys and, neglecting her husband, she became completely besotted with the second-born, Jacob, while Esau became his father's favourite. With a family thus divided, the scene was set for trouble and dissension.

It had been prophesied that Jacob would supplant the elder twin, and it was Rebekah who brought this about through a deceitful act that deeply hurt her husband and enraged the rightful heir — although Esau had already sold part of his birthright through his own carelessness. Knowing that Isaac, who was now old and blind, planned to give an irrevocable blessing to Esau as soon as he returned from the hunt, she dressed quiet, home-loving Jacob in his brother's clothes, prepared a domestic goat to taste like wild game, and covered her favourite's smooth neck and hands with the animal's pelt, so that he would feel like his hairy brother. As a result, Jacob was given the rights and privileges of the elder. On discovering that he had been supplanted, Esau began to rage, and threatened to kill his brother. So Rebekah determined to send Jacob away to stay with his uncle, back in the land she had left as a young bride.

The thought of losing her two sons in one day, one through estrangement and the other through physical separation, and the fear that she might also lose her husband, who was going on about being old and nearing death, created in her a great sadness. This was probably compounded by thoughts of her brother and the home she had left so long before, in order to marry Isaac. She must also have been struggling with a sense of guilt and loss of integrity. From the beginning, Rebekah had shown herself to be a kind and thoughtful woman, as well as strong and decisive, and her deceitful act would have greatly troubled her conscience. Added to this, she was, at the same time, having problems with her daughters-in-law, Esau's two wives.

Rebekah's Despair

Rebekah, like Isaac, had hoped that her sons would choose wives from among her own people, wives who would share her values and religious beliefs. Instead, Esau had married local Hittite women. It is not known whether Rebekah's distress came solely from her disappointment in Esau's choice, and in her having nothing in common with her daughters-in-law, or whether the two women actively goaded her. Neither do we know for how long Rebekah was depressed or how her low mood affected her. We know only that, following her deception and its disastrous outcome, she could take no more, and she told her husband that she was disgusted with living because of the Hittite women. "If Jacob takes a wife from among the women of this land, from Hittite women like these," she complained, "my life will not be worth living." [6]

Although Isaac too had been grieved by his son's choice of wives, he had possibly not thought very deeply about Esau's compromise or about his own emotional response. But now he considered and took action, ordering Jacob to go at once to his uncle and, with his help, find a wife from among his own people, a worshipper of the one true God. So Rebekah parted with her favourite, telling him that, as soon as Esau's anger had abated, she would let him know and he could return.

Rebekah's Recovery

Things didn't turn out as Rebekah had hoped. Esau continued to hate his brother and bear a grudge against her, so Jacob was unable to return. And presumably her daughters-in-law continued to plague her. But at least her outburst got through to her husband just how low she was feeling. And perhaps without the boys around, husband and wife rediscovered their former mutual love and devotion. Also, as a result of Isaac's command to Jacob, Esau realised just how displeasing his own marriages were to his father, and he took a third wife, this time from the tribe of Abraham. Whether or not Esau's conciliatory act was any comfort to Rebekah is debatable; her son had not changed in essentials, and he seemed more interested in reinstating himself with his father than with her. But this new wife may have been some consolation to her, and aided her recovery.

Life went on. Esau's wives had children, and Rebekah probably received occasional messages from Jacob, via traders, with news of his growing family. There were the usual, and some unusual, family squabbles, and Rebekah may have lived to hear of the brothers' reconciliation. But whether or not she survived the long years of estrangement, she did outlive her depression, overcoming her longing for death. In her case, there was no easy route to recovery, no pat answers. Possibly what began the healing process was the discovery that, in spite of her sadness being partially self-inflicted, she could open up to her husband and count on his love and forgiveness. Maybe also it was, along with her new daughter-in-law, the arrival of grandchildren that gave her a new lease of life, something to live for again and compensate for her former losses.

Sometimes with depression, one just has to hang on until it passes. And maybe this is how you have always coped. But it can be reassuring to know that you have not been singled out for misfortune. Life can be very cruel at times, and troubles come to us all. It also helps to know that bad times pass, and that often when least expected, life becomes rich and fulfilling again. There is no set formula for overcoming depression: like Rebekah, you have to find your own methods. But whatever way is best for you, there is one thing you can always do to speed your journey to recovery: set about repairing broken relationships, talk about your feelings, and enlist someone's support. And don't wait, as Rebekah did, until you reach the point of despair.

A POET'S LAMENT

David's Despondency

The Psalmist David was prone to depression but, unlike Rebekah, he dealt with it as and when it arose. David was a poet and musician and, like most poets, he was an idealist. So he suffered more acutely than the average person when others turned against him. This shows in Psalm 6, in which he described his grief at the destructiveness of his enemies, and his difficulty coming to terms with the realisation that they wanted to hurt him. He couldn't understand why God hadn't come to his rescue, and assumed that God must be angry with him. His anguish, doubt and sense of guilt made him so depressed that he experienced typical psychological and physical symptoms. He couldn't stop crying, he was having problems with insomnia, he felt utterly worn out, his bones ached, and he felt and looked a mess.

As an idealist, with a strong sense of right and wrong, David tended also to be easily cast down by the ills of society. In Psalm 12, for example, the main cause of David's depression was his acute awareness of political corruption. He was especially angry and grieved at the way people in authority twisted words to falsify truth, making evil seem like good, and at the resulting oppression of the weak and needy. He felt perplexed and helpless as he saw morally upright men being squeezed out of public life while worthless and base men were given positions of power, and wickedness was openly approved. David continued this theme in Psalm 13, which was a personal lament: a cry of frustration at his own helplessness, and a sob of fear that the wicked would ultimately triumph. These two psalms belong together and describe the grief and loneliness of a sensitive and caring man who wondered what on earth God was playing at. Why didn't he stop the trouble?

David's Loneliness

Job had his friends, Rebekah had her husband, but for much of the time David was alone with his questions and doubts. And his loneliness compounded his depression. When he described his emotional and physical distress in Psalm 38, David noted that, in addition to his inner torment and his enemies' taunts, his friends also were aloof. David often felt that he had no one to turn to. Even when there were people there, family and friends who shared his aims and supported him in his stand for truth and righteousness, he tended to feel isolated. His was the deep loneliness of a poet, a thoughtful and intuitive man who felt, perhaps rightly at times, that no one really understood the depths of his pain and torment. It is possible that David's sense of isolation also stemmed from childhood. The youngest of eight brothers, he was often overlooked, and his brothers treated him with contempt — which may also have created in him a deep feeling of inferiority. David certainly had a propensity to feel overwhelmed and helpless in the face of adversity, as well as alone.

David's loneliness is very evident in Psalm 63, which he wrote while in exile in the wilderness of Judah. The physical surroundings echoed his inner bleakness and thirst for love and companionship as he lamented his exclusion from the house of God in Jerusalem, and all that this represented, as well as the loss of his throne and kingdom. But in the midst of his despondency, he suddenly pictured himself back home with his own people. And his sadness turned to joy at the realisation that he wasn't alone: God was there, even in the desert, and his lovingkindness knew no bounds. David's creative ability, and the sensitivity and spiritual insight that made him so painfully aware of his physical and emotional deprivation, also enabled him to nourish his own soul, and gave him a comforting sense of assurance and hope.

David's Remedy

As a poet, composer and talented harpist, David used his creative ability to unburden himself, giving expression to painful thoughts and feelings. The very process of writing and playing music brought him relief, as did his composition of Hebrew poetry. David had a quick mind, a powerful imagination, and a very wide range of emotions, which he felt very acutely. But however destructive his thoughts, and whatever his feelings, he didn't try to hide them. He wrote them all down — hate, rage, fear, guilt, confusion — honestly describing what was going through his mind and disturbing his heart and soul.

David also used his creative ability to encourage himself. Repeatedly, throughout his psalms, David talked to himself, reminding himself that God was in control and that he would bring good out of evil. He meditated on God's faithfulness and goodness, and his reflections reassured him that, at the right moment, God would intervene. He also reminded himself that bad times pass, and that he would again feel happy and loved and wanted. Like Job, David also pondered the question of good and evil, and he too had difficulty coming up with any consistent answer. But he also recognised that, while his troubles may not have been caused by his own wrongdoing, he was nevertheless far from perfect. And he repeatedly confessed his shortcomings and sought forgiveness, so that he could move on.

Like David, you can use your creative ability as an outlet for depressed feelings, and comfort yourself with the beauty of creation and the reassurance that "God's in his heaven, all's right with the world!" It might help you to memorise some of David's psalms, or read of his exploits — or the stories of Job and Rebekah. You might also want to choose one of them as a soul friend: someone you can connect with on a deep emotional and spiritual level. Or perhaps there are other historical figures you especially identify with. This identification with another can be the first step towards enabling you to reach out to family and friends, to living human beings who can come alongside when you are down, and support you as you work at overcoming your depression — and growing beyond it.

worth moving for. Housework can wait. You will be better able to face unwelcome tasks once you have given yourself a boost by doing something you enjoy. Have a long soak in a bubble bath, go out for a walk, take up some long-forgotten embroidery or other project, cook your favourite meal.... If you are so depressed that even these are too much, at least make yourself move as far as the kitchen to make a hot drink, and find yourself something nice to eat. If you are overweight and have a tendency to go for sweet things when you are depressed, this last will not be helpful in the long run. But, the combination of moving around and boosting your blood sugar level will lessen the immediate feeling of depression, and you will then be able to go one step further by starting some form of gentle exercise.

Exercise increases the natural endorphins – painkillers – in the blood stream, so can be a great help for relieving the symptoms of mild to moderate depression. If you can't overcome your depression sufficiently to go to an aerobics class, your local gym, swimming pool, sports group or whatever appeals to you, then you can begin by exercising at home. Dancing is particularly beneficial, not only because it allows for free expression and a variety of movements, but also because music itself can lift mood, as it did, for example, with the Psalmist David. However, one has to be careful with the choice of music: choose something that is either bright and cheerful or calm and relaxing, and with lyrics that are wholesome.

Listening to pleasant music, or watching a good film, preferably a comedy or one with a happy ending, can also help alleviate the symptoms of mild to moderate depression – at least, in the short-term. And, if you are able to concentrate, read a favourite book. Or try reading the Psalms. Many of them are short and easily-digestible, as well as being uplifting, because of the writers' honest expression of their depressed feelings and accounts of how they overcame them. Being able to identify with others, through poetry, books, music and film, or losing yourself for a time in others' lives, distracting yourself from your own emotional turmoil, is always helpful. But better still, find a real live person to talk to.

There is a tendency with depression, not only to become inactive, but also to avoid company. So, in addition to praying, which involves making contact with God and telling him all the things that worry, frighten and depress you, make an effort to phone a friend. It is not always necessary or advisable to talk about your depression – although, as discussed, this can be helpful. Just re-establishing contact with the outside world and chatting about normal everyday things will, at least momentarily, give your spirits a lift. It will be even better if you can visit a friend or invite someone for coffee. Or, failing that, go where people are: the gym, a club, church or shopping centre.

If you choose to go into town – and this is much more likely to be a woman's choice – and you are not prone to over-spending, you can give yourself a boost by treating yourself to something. It needn't be anything expensive: a cup of tea and cake, a new top, some pretty underwear, an ornament for the house, or perhaps materials for something you've always wanted to make. Other means of giving yourself a boost include various types of beauty treatment – a new hairstyle, a facial, toning, etc., or different types of therapy that are mood-lifting, in particular aromatherapy. Once you have begun doing something to lift your spirits, you will be in a better position to deal with the current causes of depression.

Deal with the Current Situation

There are basically four ways of tackling current triggers of depression. The first is to do nothing. For instance, you may decide to overlook a friend's hurtful comment, accept that you can't do anything about a stroppy customer you may never see again, or conclude that it is not a good idea to challenge a boss who is prone to anger outbursts. However, the fact that you have recognised the depression triggers and made a conscious decision to do nothing about them puts you in a position of control – unless you are avoiding any action because of fear of confrontation. Choosing to do nothing is, paradoxically, a form of action, especially when you then channel your energies into dealing with the emotions aroused.

A second method of coping is to decide that the situation that is contributing to your depression is temporary and doesn't warrant changing, although you can do something to make it more tolerable while it lasts. If, for example, you have a neighbour who is being a nuisance, and you know she is planning to move, you may simply decide to avoid her as much as possible, or start letting her comments or actions wash over you. At the same time, you can work harder at monitoring her effect on you and noticing when you are over-reacting. If your depression has been triggered by a temporary bout of illness, or PMT, then part of the answer may be to indulge yourself: allow yourself time to just sit and do nothing, or perhaps ask your partner to cook your favourite meal. And in addition to availing yourself of the many treatments available, giving yourself some TLC for a change can work wonders.

The third mode of action is to do something to change a situation you are stuck with, or that you do not wish to leave. For instance, if a partner forgetting an anniversary has contributed to your depression, all that may be required is for you to tell him, in a constructive way, how you feel about his inattentiveness and arrange to celebrate at a later date. Or, if you have identified this as part of a larger picture of neglect, you can resolve to work at improving the relationship, perhaps through learning some communication skills, or going for couple counselling. If you are depressed because of a critical and overbearing work colleague from whom there is no escape, you can learn how to start being assertive, to stand up to him, telling him that you will no longer tolerate his constant put-downs. When depression is specifically related to the menopause, there are things you can do to modify its physical and emotional effects, even though you cannot turn back your biological clock. In addition to enquiring about HRT or over-the-counter medication, it is important that you recognise and deal with any past traumas and difficulties triggered by the menopause, such as not being able to have children, or feelings of failure for not having achieved your ambitions. But whatever you are going through, you can change the situation by creatively thinking about new ideas and plans for the future, and deciding to move beyond any disappointments. For instance, if depressed feelings are a result of a failed examination, you can always try again.

A fourth form of action involves stopping any harmful behaviour, such as dabbling in occult activities or bearing a grudge; or more drastically, ending a destructive relationship or permanently leaving a situation. This, of course, requires careful thought, and it will be especially frightening to have to face living alone, perhaps for the first time, or starting again in a new place. But if you tend to gravitate towards abusive, rejecting or critical people, or get stuck in unfulfilling roles, it is especially important that you make the change, otherwise you will continue repeating the patterns of depression.

Whatever action you decide to take, you will find that your having taken control of the situation will lessen any feelings of helplessness and despair. At the same time, the more you learn to control and channel your feelings, finding some constructive outlet for them, the better able you will be to take positive action. Each is dependent on the other.

Learn to Handle Feelings

In order to handle feelings effectively, it is first necessary to recognise them. This may sound self-evident, but people who are prone to depression are also likely to have developed a habit of suppressing, or even repressing, their emotions. This does not necessarily mean that they feel numb, or that they are cold and unfeeling; on the contrary, their sadness and despair can feel very intense and overwhelming. The difficulty is in recognising all the various shades of emotion, such as hurt, loneliness, anger, resentment, guilt, fear, or feeling entrapped, used, ignored, taken for granted.... It requires practice to be able to break depression down into its more specific components and, at first, you will need to constantly ask yourself, "What am I feeling?"

Having recognised your feelings, they must then have an outlet. If the predominant feelings are hurt, loneliness, being ignored or taken for granted, then perhaps allowing yourself to cry is the answer. Tears are healing, allowing a natural outflow of emotions, and they can be especially releasing in the case of delayed grief. After a bereavement you may perhaps have pushed yourself too quickly to get on with life, rather than allowing yourself to go through the grieving process, which consists of a series of emotional stages: numbness and disbelief, anger, sadness, and finally, adjustment. Failure to completely work through the stages is often an underlying factor in depression.

When the most powerful feelings are anger or resentment, these must be expressed, otherwise the anger will build up until, in one way or another, there is an explosion and someone gets hurt. Anger is often expressed destructively, through aggressive words or actions. But, since anger is a form of energy, it can be used constructively. All the reforms that have ever taken place in history have occurred because someone was angry enough to do something. This, however, is a long-term method of coping. For immediate release of anger some kind of physical activity is required, such as crying, pummelling a pillow, throwing unbreakable objects onto a bed, jogging, or working out in the gym. The golden rule of anger release is that you don't do anything that hurts yourself, other people or property.

If the main feeling contributing to your depression is guilt, then confession to God may be the only way to find immediate release. This, of course, is when it is true guilt; your having done something that has hurt someone else, or that violates your own standards – so you have therefore hurt yourself. Later, the feeling of guilt can be erased through admitting your wrongdoing to the person you harmed, and perhaps making reparation, or through resolving to change an attitude or behaviour. False guilt is not so easy to deal with. As has been noted, all the confession in the world will not release you from feelings of guilt when you haven't actually done anything wrong. In this case, you must persistently reject the guilt, and learn to recognise when someone is trying to manipulate you through playing on your emotions.

Whatever your feelings, you can also find release through talking to someone about them. This is particularly helpful if your predominant feeling is fear. Coming out into the open about your anxieties can bring an immediate sense of relief. As well as talking to people, you can also talk to God. One of the purposes of prayer is to open up our hearts to God, allowing him to bring healing and a sense of peace. But this can only happen if you are honest. For example, if you are afraid, you must openly admit your fear, rather than trying to hide it in the mistaken belief that you should not feel that way. It is human to feel fear — or guilt, anger, upset or any other emotion. Also, prayer should not be a substitute for relating to other people, especially if your main feeling is loneliness, or if you tend to avoid company. God works through people.

When you have been able to recognise and release some or all of the feelings that have contributed to your depression, and found ways of coping, you will feel lighter and freer. However, if your depression has reached the stage where you really cannot face doing anything at all, or if your self-esteem is so damaged that any attempt you make to alleviate the symptoms provides only temporary relief, then you may also need to get some professional assistance. Help can be provided in two ways: through medication and through counselling or therapy.

GET HELP

Medication

The first place to get help is your GP, who will most likely prescribe antidepressants. These do not cure depression; what they do is lessen the symptoms, making depression, and the treatment of the underlying cause, easier to deal with. They are a kind of painkiller, effective in controlling emotional pain. They do this by correcting the balance of certain chemicals in the brain. These chemicals, or neurotransmitters, have many functions, including the regulation of pain, learning and memory, eating and sleeping patterns, and moods, feelings and behaviour. Antidepressants work mainly on three neurotransmitters most implicated in depression. And whether chemical imbalance leads to depression, or the depression causes the chemical imbalance, antidepressants help to stop, and reverse, the downward spiral.

There are people who object to taking antidepressants, maintaining that they are a crutch. In many respect they are. But when you have broken your leg a crutch is very useful. It is expected, however, that a broken leg will mend and that, in time, you will no longer need your crutch. Others refuse antidepressants on the basis that they have tried them and they didn't work. But there are different kinds of antidepressants, working in different ways. So, if you have had difficulty with any medication in the past, discuss this with your doctor. Also, bear in mind that usually two or three weeks are needed before antidepressants start taking effect, and that they need to be taken in the dosage prescribed, and for the time prescribed.

Counselling and Therapy

In conjunction with, or instead of, medication, help can be obtained through counselling or psychotherapy. If there is a counsellor at your GP practice, you will normally be able to have six sessions on the NHS. Otherwise, you will probably have to pay. But look on this as an investment: you are contributing to your own life and future. And in the long run it will probably be well worth it. You will be able to discover trained counsellors or psychotherapists in your area through your GP, Yellow Pages, or through contacting counselling organisations, such as the Association of Christian Counsellors (ACC), the British Association for Counselling and Psychotherapy (BACP), or the UK Council for Psychotherapists (UKCP).

There are many theoretical models for counselling, and counsellors work in different ways, depending on their training and current focus. It is impossible in a book of this length to discuss all the various schools of thought, such as Gestalt, which focuses on the whole person, and Transactional Analysis, which looks at the parent, adult and child parts of the self and how these affect ways of thinking and acting. Instead, we will focus on the three main streams of psychology: Cognitive-Behavioural, Humanistic (or Rogerian) and Psychodynamic.

A counsellor trained in Cognitive-Behavioural Therapy will focus on the here and now, rather than the past. This type of treatment can be very useful for increasing understanding of depression and teaching coping methods. In particular, a cognitive counsellor will be able to help you recognise and change maladaptive ways of thinking and irrational expectations, all of which feed and perpetuate depression. But there will probably be no exploration of the underlying factors, certainly not the unconscious ones, and little help in working through painful childhood experiences.

By contrast, counsellors who are trained in Humanistic methods believe that people don't need teaching; they have the answers to life's problems within themselves. And they help clients get in touch with, and actualise themselves; that is, realise their full potential. This mode of treatment also has its strengths and weaknesses. Humanistic counsellors emphasise the importance of care, empathy and congruence, and so can provide the type of nurturing that depressed people usually need. But with severe depression, it may not be possible to respond to their very non-directive methods. And, like Cognitive-Behaviourists, they tend not to look at the root causes of depression.

Psychodynamic counsellors focus on the clients' inner worlds and seek to discover the causes of emotional dysfunction, and to bring healing. In this respect, this type of treatment is the most helpful for recurring clinical depression. But the main disadvantage is that some psychodynamic counsellors tend to explore irrational thoughts, feelings and fantasies at the expense of rational thought and will, and to undermine the importance of external reality: what is happening in the client's personal world of home, work and society as a whole.

Many counsellors nowadays use an integrated approach, and adapt their methods to suit individual clients and meet specific needs. If you decide on private counselling or therapy, then shop around. Find a practitioner whom you can relate to and trust; enquire about his or her training and current methods of working. And don't give up. When depression has arisen because of childhood abuse or neglect, it can take a long time to work through the pain, make sense of it all, and put it behind you. You are not going to change in a few short sessions what has taken years to build up.

However, whether or not you feel that you need, or are ready for, professional help, you can, with the help of this book, and especially the next chapter, do more than simply learn how to manage depression. You can begin the process of growing beyond the darkness and despair into the light.

5

GROWING BEYOND DEPRESSION

LET GO OF THE PAST

Retrace your Steps

At the start of this book, depression was defined as the soul hurting. It was also pointed out that a normal, reactive depression can become more severe if there are old wounds that have never properly healed. Growing beyond depression, whether it is an isolated and frightening experience or a recurring blight on your life, involves more than simply understanding depression and learning some coping mechanisms. It involves going back into the past, tending to the old wounds and facilitating healing. It also necessitates recognising and changing the destructive patterns of thinking and behaving that lead to depression. Finally, it requires that you work at improving your self-esteem, making your life more interesting and fulfilling, and setting goals, so that you always have something to look forward to.

Since the focus of this chapter is on recurring depression, the greater emphasis will be on working through the pain of childhood abuse or rejection. However, as has been discussed, the root causes may be unrelated to upbringing. An underlying cause may, for example, be the death of a parent, or their separation or divorce, a bad experience at school, or a particularly devastating accident or debilitating illness. Something relatively minor can lead to a propensity to depression if it occurred at a critical time in one's development. Or there could be a series of minor happenings, all combining to erode one's sense of self-worth. But since the effects are more or less the same, this chapter is applicable even if your childhood was essentially a happy one. We all have parts of ourselves where psychological and spiritual growth has been halted or slowed down. We all need to grow into the light. And we begin by retracing our steps, going back as far as necessary to where the growth was first impaired.

Remember the Facts and Feelings

Not only has everyone experienced past hurts and traumas, everyone also has a tendency to either discount, minimise or dismiss them, reasoning that, since they are in the past, they are no longer relevant. But the soul is eternal: in the depth of the human psyche there is no past, present or future. This is why things that happened years ago can pop up when least expected and hold you back all over again. And this is why, in order to grow beyond depression, you have to go back into the past and understand where, when and how the emotional growth was halted. And this means, first of all, allowing yourself to remember the facts of any mistreatment or trauma. You can do this in several ways. You can start a journal, making notes of the major events in your life, in some sort of chronological order. Or you can simply allow yourself time and space in which your mind can wander, selecting and connecting different aspects of your past.

If you think you may have repressed painful memories, you will probably need professional help to bring them to the surface. A skilled counsellor or psychotherapist will be acutely aware of timing and will not force memory recall, so you needn't fear being overwhelmed by your impressions and feelings. Also, with a skilled practitioner you needn't fear having a "false memory" of abuse. These don't appear out of the blue. There is usually some remembrance, although it may be hazy, perhaps no more than a vague sense of something bad having happened. And any newly surfaced memories will be consistent with conscious thoughts and feelings. So, to a large extent, you will be able to judge for yourself whether or not they are real.

It is important to remember, not only the facts of past abuse or trauma, but also the feelings that went with them, and to understand why they arose and how they are affecting you now. You cannot work through feelings and leave them behind if you are denying their existence or relevance, kidding yourself perhaps that, although it might be necessary to recall incidents and situations, your feelings have long since passed away and should be left alone. Severe or recurring depression is proof that, in some form or other, those emotions do live on. The predominant feelings associated with an unhappy childhood, or any kind of psychological damage – confusion, worthlessness, anger, guilt and fear – particularly need to be addressed.

Release the Pain

Having faced up to and made sense of past hurts and trauma, and allowed the feelings to surface, you then need to let them out. You can do this, first, by talking about them. This is not with the intention of allocating blame, but in order to express thoughts and impressions that, consciously or unconsciously, have been going round and round in your head for years. Putting hurt into words is releasing, especially if the person you choose to tell is able to listen, understand and be supportive. And getting things out into the open will enable you to stand back and see the whole picture.

You will probably also need to give vent to your feelings through action – as discussed in the previous chapter. You can think of this venting as a first-aid measure: it is not a long-term method of coping. It may be sufficient to merely allow yourself to cry, or to express anger and regret to someone who is able to contain your emotions and help you feel safe with them. Releasing your long-buried memories, thoughts and feelings is analogous to draining a wound, so that the edges can come together and repair themselves.

Allow Wounds to Heal

If the soul-hurt that constitutes depression has arisen because of childhood abuse, the hurt goes very deep – hence the need for draining. It is also necessary to clean the wound, which may have become contaminated by a build-up of self-criticism, anger, false guilt and generalised fear. This involves letting go of the negative thoughts and feelings that have developed as a result of the original injury. Wounds cannot heal if you keep putting yourself down, telling yourself that you are no good, that you will never amount to anything, that you are fat, ugly, or whatever; or if you keep stirring up resentment, or wallowing in self-pity or self-blame.

You can begin the process of cleansing by starting to recognise and accept your positive qualities. Ask God to help you find the essentially good person inside, the person he created, values and loves. You also need to release your anger, especially if this normal, healthy emotion has turned into bitterness and a desire for revenge or restitution. Bitterness does not harm the person you perceive to be an enemy; it harms you, keeping the old wounds open and liable to re-infection. You also have to relinquish false guilt. So stop blaming yourself for things that were not your fault, and question any tendency to be super-responsible, taking on the ills of the world. Finally, start losing your fear, through facing up to it, recognising who or what you were originally afraid of, and not allowing yourself to generalise this fear to others. To grow beyond depression, you have to stop bearing a grudge, or carrying the weight of self-inflicted guilt and unnecessary fear. You have to let go.

Letting go is the essence of forgiveness. And, for there to be full forgiveness, there has to be full awareness of the wrong done to you. This is why you have to remember the past and put the responsibility where it belongs. Forgiveness is not the same as denying, excusing, or tolerating. You don't have to keep putting yourself back into a situation where you know you will be repeatedly hurt. This will not only cause a constant re-opening of old wounds; it will also deepen them, making them worse. If there has been a lot of hurt, you may have to forgive in stages, a bit at a time. But the more you are able to forgive, the more you will heal.

The soul, like the body, can repair itself, as long as the wounds are kept clean and there is the provision of rest and care. The healing of memories is speeded up when there is also an experience of being nurtured, or cared for; being fed with thoughts and ideas that are healthy and enriching, building you up into the person you were meant to be. This nurturing may come through a counsellor, spouse, partner, friend.... The deep knowledge that you are unconditionally loved and accepted for who you are is a balm to the soul, soothing old hurts and aiding recovery. And as you start opening yourself up to love, believing in it, accepting it and rejoicing in it, you will find it easier to remove the defences that you have built up over the years, shutting yourself in and other people and God out.

COME OUT OF HIDING

Recognise the Defences

Developing a set of coping mechanisms, or defences, is essential when you are under attack. The problem is, defences that have been built up in order to cope with emotional trauma tend to persist long after the danger has passed. So, rather than protecting you, they trap you, holding you back so that you are unable to grow and develop into the person you want to be. In order to remove the defences, you first have to remember and recognise how and why you developed your own particular survival skills. Then you need to recognise and identify the type of defence you hide behind most frequently.

A common defence mechanism is denial. Children who are repeatedly hurt often cope by telling themselves that it isn't happening. Imaginative children especially may deny the reality of abuse or rejection through daydreaming. They will picture themselves elsewhere, in different circumstances with different parents. In severe cases, they may live in a world of their own making, losing complete touch with reality. By adulthood, the use of this defence may have become so automatic that the ability to recognise danger is diminished, or even lost. If denial is your defence, then you are at risk of putting yourself back into abusive situations, allowing yourself to be made use of, walked over, put down, constantly criticised, or sexually or physically abused all over again. In other words, you are in danger of creating the very circumstances that lead to depression.

A defence similar to denial is shut-down. When abuse of any kind is ongoing, children learn to switch off their normal emotional and physical response to pain. So, they grow up to be very stoical and may even have masochistic tendencies. As adults, they are likely to be emotionally hard and cold on the outside, while knowing – if they haven't completely shut down – that inside there is a soft, hurting person trying to get out. The price of shut-down is high; you are likely to end up losing touch with yourself and being cut off from others, unable to recognise or respond to genuine love. You will be shut up in a fortress of your own making, unaware that the danger has passed.

The defence of withdrawal similarly cuts a person off from the outside world, making him unable to respond to others' offers of friendship and love. A child withdraws because it isn't safe to be seen, physically or emotionally. He is trying to be invisible. By adulthood, he will tend to disappear into the woodwork, to shrink from social contact, even when there is a longing to be noticed, responded to, and cared for. If you tend to withdraw, you might occasionally find yourself reacting with aggression, either to express anger, get attention – even if it hurts – or gain a sense of control. Both withdrawal and aggression also have their price, which is loneliness: a sense of isolation, of being different and not really belonging. The real world continues to be a threatening place, even when the threat has been removed.

Sometimes the defence used is perfectionism. This usually arises when it is impossible to win a parent's love or approval, or when a parent has unrealistic expectations and sets impossible standards. The child often keeps on trying, driving himself harder and harder in the hope that one day there will be the longed-for response. By adulthood, he will have developed a compulsion to strive for general recognition and acclaim. On the other hand, the child may give up, using instead the defence of apathy, which again is continued into adult life. Both of these defences – a drive to be perfect or a couldn't-care-less attitude – will hinder your ability to cope with life. There will be an on-going attempt to sign a peace treaty that has already been signed, or to pretend indifference to a foe that has long since become an ally.

As you become increasingly aware of your own particular defences, you then have to start removing them. But first, you have to feel safe. And you cannot begin to feel safe until the threats and dangers of the past really have become things of the past. Therefore, as you take down your defences, you have to continue working at resolving and letting go of past hurts and traumas, and the feelings that went with them.

Remove the Defences

Defences can be thought of in terms of armour, as well as fortresses. Medieval armour was very useful for battles, but it couldn't be worn all the time. Its weight was such that, if a knight fell off his horse, he needed someone to lift him back on again. The weight of your defences is a large component in your tendency to be cast down by depression. However, since armour does have its uses, you should not abandon it completely – life does have a habit of attacking us when least expected. And it is important that you remove it just one piece at a time. Don't leave yourself feeling so vulnerable that you can't cope.

If denial is your defence, then you will need to start facing up to the reality of what was and is. If you daydream excessively, start taking control of your mind and focus on what is actually happening in your life. Only then can you change the things you don't like, and move on. But daydreaming, like night dreams, enables you to get in touch with unconscious memories and motives, and can be very productive and creative. Daydreaming is also a way of relaxing the mind, so it should by no means be eliminated. The secret is to get the balance right.

If you tend to shut down feelings, then you will need to work especially hard at allowing yourself to feel. Begin by asking yourself when you are down, "What am I feeling?" Then label each of the specific feelings, such as rejection, disappointment, betrayal.... Allow yourself to cry, rather than telling yourself not to be silly; or admit that you are hurt rather than telling yourself to just get on with things. You cannot truly move on until you are able to open up to other people and new experiences, which means first being open to yourself.

If your defence is to withdraw, then start moving out towards others, going where people are and learning to form healthy relationships. Have faith in your own beliefs and values and start sharing them, whilst also being open to others' opinions. If you use aggression as a coping mechanism, then you will need to learn how to recognise, constructively express and channel anger. You will find the book in this series, *Beyond Anger: Growing into calm,* especially helpful with this.

If you are a perfectionist, then, as with daydreaming, work at getting the balance right. In some situations it is essential to be perfect. But it is not vital to hoover every day, make the beds before you go out, or never make a clerical error. In other words, allow yourself to be human. This not only makes life far less stressful, but also prevents the onset of apathy and depression when you have failed to live up to your own unrealistic expectations.

As you come out from behind your defences and remove your armour, you will find yourself learning to trust people, rather than seeing everyone as your abuser or critic. You will also find it easier to trust your own instincts regarding others' reliability. At first you will make mistakes and expose yourself at times when you should really be covering yourself. But in time you will learn to live without your defences. And with past encumbrances removed, you will travel through life with less effort, and be able to make it much more interesting and rewarding.

MAKE THE PRESENT MORE INTERESTING

Develop Healthy Relationships

Psychological and spiritual growth and enrichment occur within the context of relationships: we need people. Without them we not only feel isolated and abandoned, we also stagnate. So, in order to live life to the full, you need to work at developing a healthy relationship with yourself, others, God and the entire created world.

First, start getting to know and like yourself. As well as acknowledging your good points, identify those things you don't like about yourself and start changing them. Do you, for example, dislike yourself because you are bad tempered, a misery, boring, not much fun, or is it because of the way you look, or think you look? You may need to work at improving your self-esteem by recognising how others have put you down and how you are repeating the patterns, and then start being kinder to yourself, giving yourself praise where it is due, and lots of encouragement. At the same time, you can work at discovering your own beliefs, values and interests and enhancing your creative ability. (This topic is pursued in depth in the book by this author, *Self-esteem: The way of humility*.) The more you like and appreciate yourself, the better able you will be to relate to others.

Forming relationships with others necessitates more than being able to function socially. It involves the ability to get close to people. Those who are depressed tend to have difficulty in this area, because of the defences. You cannot get close to someone if you are walking around in armour! Closeness means letting people see you as you really are, and this requires trust. As with everything else, start slowly, first enlarging the number of your acquaintances, then finding friends with whom you can share interests or hobbies. Then, start letting people see when you are hurt or in need, and allow them to help, whether emotionally through support and empathy, or practically: providing transport, doing your shopping when you are ill, or meeting your needs in some other way.

In its most general sense, forming a healthy relationship with God and the entire created world involves getting in touch with your creative, aesthetic self and opening yourself up to the beauty and wonder of the world around. It also means experiencing the healing that comes, not only from nature's inherent loveliness, but also from the sense of being in synch with the rhythm of the universe. More specifically, forming a relationship with God necessitates removing the defences that have shut him out, and opening yourself up to his love, so that you can experience its transforming power. It is more than knowing about God, through going to church, praying, or reading your Bible, although all of these are helpful. It means getting to know what God is like and allowing him to be a friend and companion; someone who can assist you to find the happiness he intended you to have.

When you can live at peace with yourself, other people and God, you will be better able to cope with the ups and downs of life, and the enhanced relationships will make life richer and more fulfilling. At the same time, you can help yourself grow beyond depression by finding more specific ways of improving your life, beginning at home.

Enhance your Home Life

If you are prone to depression it is also likely, if you are with a partner and have children, that your family has been neglected. And possibly a stale, boring relationship has, in turn, contributed to the depression, causing a vicious, downward spiral. If you are severely depressed you will, with this as with everything else, need to go slowly. First, ask yourself what is lacking. Has work or the demands of children taken over to such an extent that you and your partner have no time for each other? Has your sex life become routine and unexciting, or even non-existent? Have you become lazy, not wanting to make the effort to go out or invite friends for coffee or meals? And what about your children? Have you become so depressed that you are no longer able to enjoy them?

If you answered yes to any of these, then your life is out of balance and you need to reorganise it so that you have time and space for yourself, you and your partner, and your family as a whole. It may need only a few minor adjustments, like periodically turning the TV off and talking to each other, bringing some romance into your marriage – candlelit meals, inexpensive presents, and those three important words, "I love you." You may need to reschedule your work so that you can socialise more, play games with the children, and arrange picnics and outings. Planning for regular times of fun and relaxation with the family is essential if you are to permanently keep depression at bay.

Improve your Working Life

It may be that your life is unfulfilling because of your employment, and if this is the case, then a reappraisal of your work life is also called for. Begin by asking yourself some questions. Have you found your niche in life? Are you doing the job you really want to do? If not, ask yourself why you have got yourself into a rut. Is it because your job is convenient, it pays the mortgage, or because you are afraid of trying anything new? In order to move beyond depression you have to be in a job that gives you a sense of your own worth, that creates interest and enables you to fulfil your potential. If there is need of a change, again go slowly, and be realistic. You may not be able to make any alterations at present, but you can start thinking about what you would really like to do and begin heading in that direction.

If you are basically happy in your job but feel that you are not being stimulated enough, then think of ways of improving the work situation. Perhaps there is the possibility of a transfer to another department, or maybe you can ask for more challenging assignments. And make life more interesting by trying new things outside of the workplace: start a new project at home, take up a hobby, attend evening classes or college courses, join a club or church. Or maybe you can spare a few hours each week for voluntary work. This could also provide some useful experience, paving the way for you to realise your career dreams, as well as being fun.

Learn how to Play

People who are depressed, and especially those who have experienced childhood abuse, find it particularly difficult to play. This means doing things simply because they are fun, not because they lead to a goal of any kind. Play is by its nature spontaneous, and is an antidote to stress as well as depression. When life has a healthy balance of work and play, then depression has far less chance to take hold.

Play for you may simply mean allowing yourself to settle down for an hour or so with a cup of coffee and a good book – even when you haven't finished the housework. It might mean putting some music on and dancing, or singing, memorising poetry, extracts of Shakespeare or the Psalms. It might involve taking yourself off to the seaside for the day, or into the country, or visiting a museum or art gallery. But in order to grow beyond depression, rather than simply giving your feelings a quick occasional boost, you must develop the habit of playing, keeping a constant check on yourself so that you don't drift back into your old habits of working round the clock, day in and day out. As you learn to play, as well as developing healthy relationships and enriching your present life at home and work, you will find yourself also becoming more hopeful about the future.

SET GOALS FOR THE FUTURE

Plan Short-term Goals

Having goals keeps hope alive, and it implies that you have sufficient faith in yourself to reach those goals. It is important that, as well as long-term goals, you also have short-term easily reachable ones. These can be very simple, like plucking up courage to ask someone to go shopping with you, completing a decorating project, writing a short story or poem, attempting a painting, or taking up music again. It may involve doing something you have always wanted to do but never had the courage to try, like going horse riding or having a holiday abroad. Or it could be more ambitious; something that requires a period of time to achieve, such as making preliminary enquiries about a new job, whether paid or voluntary, or completing a short course of study. With every achievement, however small, your self-esteem will be given a boost and you will be encouraged to keep going forward, to create and realise future dreams.

Have Long-term Goals

A common feeling with depression is that there is nothing to look forward to; that life will continue with the same unchanging monotony for ever and ever. For this reason it is essential that you also have a long-term goal. This may be something that you can begin working towards immediately, using your short-term goals as markers on the road to your ultimate destination. Examples are getting a university degree, or saving for a holiday or new house. Or it may be something that is dependent on time, such as starting a project once the children are at school, or taking up a new hobby when you retire. Your aim may be more concerned with personal development, such as achieving a certain weight, or becoming less angry and more caring. But whatever your goal, you need to constantly keep it in mind, picturing yourself realising your dreams and fulfilling your potential.

The suggestions in this book for understanding and overcoming depression can be considered as short-term goals; steps towards your ultimate aim of growing beyond depression into the light. If you are currently depressed, begin by choosing one or two practical suggestions from Chapters 4 and 5 that you can work on immediately. Then gradually take on increasingly more challenges. At the same time, start taking down your defences and allow others to give you the help and support you need. Above all, let God be in your past, present and future. And, inspired by those biblical characters who struggled with depression, start opening yourself up to God's healing power and love.

God himself is light and the creator of light. Ultimately, it is he alone who can take you beyond depression, not by providing you with simplistic answers, or by demanding that you immediately banish your own darkness, but by gently leading you, step by step, out of your black tunnel or barren wilderness into a future that is bright with promise.

Endnotes

1 Hebrews 9.27
2 Ephesians 4.26
3 Psalm 55.6-8
4 Jonah 4.3
5 Job 3.1-3
6 Genesis 27.46

Silvertree Grobooks

Jennifer Minney

Beyond depression: Growing into light
ISBN: 0-9538446-3-3

Beyond fear: Growing into faith
ISBN: 0-9538446-5-X

Beyond stress: Growing into serenity
ISBN: 0-9538446-4-1

Using Bible characters as case studies, each book discusses signs and symptoms, current triggers and deep-rooted causes, and provides guidelines for overcoming the immediate effects. The emotional difficulties are also viewed in the context of the entire person, and the reader is helped to find healing from past traumas and begin changing destructive patterns of thinking and behaviour; to move beyond the problem towards spiritual and psychological wholeness.

All titles £3.50

Coming soon:

Beyond anger: Growing into calm
Beyond marital discord: Growing into love
Beyond parenting chaos: Growing into harmony

Also by Jennifer Minney

Self-esteem: The way of humility

This thoughtful book promotes the development of self-esteem on the basis of one's identity in God, through creation and redemption. This foundation, it explains, is essential for creating a respect for self that is humble and grateful, and that leads to a more responsible and effective stewardship of one's gifts and abilities.

The author, a counsellor with a BA (Hons) in Psychology, and more than twenty years experience of helping people with low self-esteem, draws also on her Bible college, nursing and midwifery training to explore and discuss five aspects of the self: body, soul, spirit, heart and mind. With each, there is a survey of common misconceptions and problems, with guidelines for overcoming them.

£5.95 **ISBN: 0-9538446-2-5**

Will Jesus kick my ball back?

The amazing story of an adoption that should have been impossible, of cerebral palsy, and a child whose avid curiosity and irrepressible giggles have made him a joy to many.

It is also the story of the author's spiritual and psychological journey, from a background of abuse and rejection, through years of infertility, to a place of trust in God's goodness, even when his long-promised child turns out to be severely brain-damaged. It is a story of learning to open up to God's love and experiencing him, no longer as rigid and punitive, but as a loving, approachable Father with whom it is safe to be oneself, to be child-like — to play.

The two stories blend as mother and child grow together, developing their full potential as she learns to love herself and a child whom a neurologist had written off.

This book has had a profound impact on those who have read it, provoking laughter, producing tears, challenging, uplifting and enriching the soul. It is a book that is hard to put down.

£6.95 **ISBN: 0-9538446-0-9**

All Silvertree titles are available from bookshops or can be purchased (postage free in UK) direct from:

Silvertree Publishing
PO Box 2768
Yeovil
Somerset BA22 8XZ

Become a Silvertree Book Agent

If you found this book helpful, why not become a Silvertree Book Agent, and so benefit others whilst also earning money for yourself, your church, or your favourite charity?

For full details, send an s.a.e. to the above address.